Cooperative Learning

GETTING STARTED

BY
SUSAN S. ELLIS
AND SUSAN F. WHALEN

New York • Toronto • London • Aukland • Sydney

Cover design by Vincent Ceci
Design by Joel White
Cover photograph by Richard Hutchings

ISBN 0-590-49092-3

12 11 10 9 8 7 6 5 4 3 2   1 2 3 4 5/9
                                                      31

Printed in the U.S.A.

For Harold and Chad,

who keep teaching me how to cooperate

S.S.E.

For John, Gwyn, and Megan,

who are my spirit and strength

S.F.W.

Contents

Acknowledgments

Every book is a cooperative venture—especially this one. We are indebted to Roger Johnson, David Johnson and Edythe Johnson Holubec for introducing us to cooperative learning and for making it possible for us—and many other teachers and administrators in the Greenwich Public Schools—to become enthusiastic users of this strategy. We are particularly grateful to them for their continued support of our efforts and for their friendship.

And thanks to all the Greenwich administrators who provided the support that enabled so many Greenwich teachers to become effective users and enthusiastic advocates of cooperative learning, especially former superintendent of schools Ernie Fleishman, the "godfather" of this book.

We appreciate the support Susan Whalen has received from her colleagues at the Glenville School, particularly her fifth-grade team, Judy Tattar and Donna Borst. Thanks, also, to Glenville's principal, Tom Brown; teacher leader, Margo Neale; school secretary, Pat Finnegan; and the custodial staff, without whom the Glenville Cooperative Learning Days could never have happened. And, of course, thanks to the Glenville students.

Many of our colleagues in the Greenwich Public Schools have contributed to our understanding of how cooperative learning really works. We wish there were space to acknowledge them all by name.

We give special thanks to Peggy Jorgensen, Judy Freier, Sue Pascucci, Jeanne Igneri, Marge Nielsen, Sue Snyder, Rae Baczek, John Harmon, Janet MacKenzie, Janet Clausi, Carolyn Pagnano, Janess Coffina, Paula Madey, Gail Montgomery, Peggy McLaughlin, Florence Schorow, Bonnie Drinkwater Butera, Dwight Wall, Traci Brandon, Ann Mason, Linda Shirley, Jill Bleemer, Joanne Zammit, Caralliene Westbrook, Anne Baltren, Arline Lomazzo, Marilyn Maxwell, Dick Campbell, Terese Fuller, Anne Gilhuly, Joel Adelberg, Ruth Lindegren, Barbara Johnson, Alice Ell, the late Ellen Moness, Karen Nagy, Martha Awdziewicz, Jeanne Coombs, Beth Hughes, Lee Spong, Sandi Mackenzie, Rose Cosentino, Ann Lindemann, Jane Gartman Kahn, Brenda Macri, Jean Bennet, Bob Sleath, Barbara Sullivan, Joe Patrick, and Carole Quinn for letting themselves be observed using cooperative learning in their classrooms or for sharing their favorite cooperative learning lessons with us.

As we worked on this book, Brenda Friedler, Suzanne Whalen, and Nancy Gallo were good listeners and encouragers for Susan Whalen. (See Chapter 5.) Kate Waters and Muriel Laskin provided the same essential support for Susan Ellis.

Our most enduring and enthusiastic support—in this as in all ventures—has come from our husbands, Charley Ellis and John Whalen.

Introduction

During my years of exploring, teaching, and writing about cooperative learning I have developed a firm conviction: two heads *are* better than one. So when Scholastic asked me to write a book about cooperative learning, I answered, "Sure, if I can write it with a teacher."

Working on this book with Susan Whalen was truly a cooperative venture. At each step in the process Susan provided concrete suggestions based on her own classroom experiences in grades 3 and 5 and the experiences of her colleagues on the Glenville Cooperative Learning Team. Her feedback was invaluable, both when she suggested changes and when she said, "I think it's terrific!"

Our partnership illustrates the value of cooperative work. We each contributed our own knowledge, skills, and experiences, and together we created a book that neither of us could have produced on her own. And we provided each other with essential encouragement and support throughout the process.

As you read this book and think about ways to use cooperative learning with your students, we hope you'll find colleagues who will collaborate with you. Try to develop a support system—perhaps another teacher on your grade level or one whose classroom is nearby. Share your plans for a cooperative learning lesson—or better yet, plan a lesson together. Talk out difficulties you think may arise and see if together you can develop some strategies for avoiding them.

It's important to get emotional support, too. When things go particularly well, it helps to have a colleague who will cheer your successes. And when you run into difficulty, you'll want someone to encourage you to keep trying and to brainstorm possible solutions to the problem you've encountered.

Not only will your cooperative efforts with a colleague make your own learning easier, but they'll also serve as a good model for your students. You'll be demonstrating that you really believe that two heads are better than one.

Susan S. Ellis

1

An Introduction To Cooperative Learning

"What are cooperative learning groups? How are they different from the small groups I'm now using?"

C ooperative learning has become a hot topic in education these past few years. Teachers in elementary, middle, and high schools are experimenting with cooperative learning groups, seeing if their students will learn more, learn better, or simply enjoy learning.

If you've read about cooperative learning in education magazines, or if you have a friend or colleague who is raving about this "new" strategy, you've probably wondered what all the excitement is about. Perhaps you have asked, "Is cooperative learning really new? What does it look like in action? How are cooperative groups different from the small groups I'm already using for various projects?"

Cooperative Learning Is an Old Idea

Cooperative learning is *not* new. Back at the turn of the century John Dewey was encouraging teachers to put students into groups to investigate and solve problems. In the 1960s Morton Deutsch (like Dewey, a professor at Teachers College, Columbia University) began his own work investigating and promoting cooperative learning models, particularly as strategies for helping students learn to solve conflicts.

Research on cooperative learning continued throughout the 1970s, and in the 1980s several professors began to receive attention for developing models that put the best of their learning from research into practice. Roger and David Johnson at the University of Minnesota, Robert Slavin at The Johns Hopkins University in Baltimore, Maryland, Neil Davidson at the University of Maryland, and Spencer Kagan, formerly at the University of California at Riverside and now director of resources for teachers in San Juan Capistrano, California, are the best known of this group. Our work has been with Roger and David Johnson, and most of the ideas we share in this book reflect their approach to cooperative learning.

Many others have contributed to the growing body of research and practical experience with cooperative learning, including Nancy and Theodore Graves, Elliot Aronson, Nancy Schniedewind, Schlomo and Yeal Sharan, and Patricia Roy. At the end of this book we've supplied a bibliography of books, articles, audiovisual materials, and teacher materials to help you continue your exploration of cooperative learning.

What's New and Different About Cooperative Learning

If cooperative learning is an old idea that resurfaced vigorously in the 1980s, it is also a new idea to most teachers, because cooperative learning groups are very different from the usual small groups found in classrooms.

Before we describe the essential characteristics of cooperative learning groups, however, we need to talk about the three kinds of settings teachers can create in their classrooms. These settings all help students develop particular attitudes toward other students and the teacher and foster expectations for how learning will take place.

Settings for Learning:
Competitive, Individualistic, or Cooperative

The first setting, and perhaps the most familiar, is *competitive*. In a competitive classroom, children walk into the room the first day of school and ask themselves, "Who's going to be the best student this year?" or "Whom do I have to beat if I want to be best?" or "Who's going to make me look stupid?" In secondary schools the question is often, "Who's going to skew the curve and make it hard for me to get a good grade?"

The motto for competitive classrooms is, If you win, I lose; if I win, you lose. Students compete with each other for scarce resources: grades, teacher recognition and praise, prized jobs, extra recess—whatever currency the teacher has found will "motivate" students to work.

In a competitive classroom students see each other as obstacles rather than as sources of help and support. Do you remember hoping that someone else would get an answer wrong so that you would have a chance to be called on and be right? Or hoping you *wouldn't* be called on because others would silently cheer if you made a mistake?

It's obvious that competition is hard on the students who frequently or always "lose." Many come to see themselves as losers and opt out of the education game. Some of these students derive their sense of self-esteem from sports or artistic activities; others gain recognition by being a clown or by "acting out" and getting into trouble.

What may be less obvious is that competition hurts winners, too. Students who win prizes for their work often worry about whether they can continue to outshine everyone else. They fear failure and the loss of love or approval they expect it will bring. And while they're winning, they're often ostracized by the other students—labeled a brain or a nerd or a brownie. By the time they get to middle school, many students would rather be caught dead than have one of these labels.

Competition also has negative effects on the children we call the salt of the earth. These are the "average" children: they don't act out to get attention, but often they have good social skills, get along well with others, and are quite successful in life—once they're out of school. A competitive setting doesn't allow them any opportunity to shine.

Is competition in classrooms always bad? No, of course not. In fact, competition can be fun—provided a few rules are followed:

- Have students compete with others who are on the same ability level.
- Maximize the number of winners.

"In today's typical classroom, each student works alone. He or she is told 'Keep your eyes on your own work; don't share; don't compare; don't talk; don't help.' This approach is totally contrary to the basic human need to belong. It also ignores the need for personal importance. How can you feel important if you're working by yourself? Who recognizes you? Who talks to you?...Most of us feel important only as members of a team."

Pauline B. Gough. "The Key To Improving Schools: An Interview With William Glasser." *Phi Delta Kappan,* May 1987. Page 659.

13

- Make sure it's not a life-or-death situation, like a test or a final exam.
- Use competition for fun, review, or for a change of pace.

Teachers are well aware of many of the negative effects of competition, and most teachers try to minimize it in their classrooms. One popular noncompetitive approach is *individualized learning.*

In an individualistic setting students don't have to worry about who might make them look bad. They work alone, at their own pace, and compete (if they choose to) against themselves to see how much they can accomplish. Their only interactions with other students are at nonacademic times—during recess, at lunch, or in the gym.

The motto of an individualistic classroom could be, We're all in this alone. Students don't look to their peers for help or support; the teacher is their primary resource. And here lies the main drawback of individualized instruction: *learning is primarily a social activity.*

As Piaget demonstrated, much of our most important learning comes through our interactions with others. If students have only their own ideas, reactions, and questions to bring to a text or a worksheet or a problem, their learning is not as rich as it could be if they had access to others' ideas. In addition, psychologists have identified an important part of learning called *oral rehearsal.* This is the opportunity to think out loud and learn by listening to ourselves discuss with others what we think.

And besides, working alone most or all of the time is lonely and, ultimately, boring. Certainly students need to be able to work independently, but for most of their learning they will benefit from working and interacting with others.

This brings us to the third kind of setting teachers can create: a *cooperative classroom.* In such a setting students learn that they can count on their classmates to help when they need help, listen when they have something to contribute, and celebrate their accomplishments. Instead of seeing the teacher as the major resource, students in cooperative classrooms come to view their peers as important and valuable sources of knowledge.

The motto for a cooperative classroom is, We sink or swim together. And here we come to the first of the essential characteristics of cooperative learning: *positive interdependence.* Teachers must structure cooperative learning activities so that students are genuinely interdependent. No member of a group can be successful unless all are successful.

This means that it doesn't do Sally any good to finish all the math problems on the group's worksheet and ignore Will, who can't figure out how she knew to divide first and then multiply. And Robert can't write out all the answers to the social studies questions without making sure that Claire and Michael understand those answers and agree with him. And Levandra won't win any points for learning all the new vocabulary words if her partner Denise doesn't learn them, too.

14

Hand in hand with positive interdependence goes the second essential characteristic of cooperative learning: *individual accountability*. Every student must know that she or he will be held accountable for learning the material. No one is allowed to hitchhike or opt out of the group's task.

All cooperative learning models share these two elements. What the Johnsons have added is an emphasis on teaching students the social skills they need to function well in cooperative groups. After all, we don't simply hand first graders a book, say "read," and expect them immediately to acquire that complex skill. Nor should we put students into groups and say "cooperate" and expect them to know how to work together.

In order for cooperative groups to succeed, teachers need to do three things:

- monitor their students' behavior while they're working in groups;
- give their students feedback on their use of social skills and help them become conscious of their use of those skills; and
- intervene to teach needed skills whenever appropriate.

Cooperative Learning vs. Small Group Activities

At the beginning of this chapter we assumed that you were wondering how cooperative learning groups are different from the small-group activities most teachers use in their classrooms. Here's a chart that outlines the main differences.

COOPERATIVE GROUPS	SMALL GROUPS
Positive interdependence: we sink or swim together. Face-to-face oral interaction.	No interdependence. Students often work on their own, occasionally checking their answers with other students.
Individual accountability: each person must master the material.	Hitchhiking. Some students let others do most or all of the work.
Teacher teaches social skills needed for successful group work.	Social skills not systematically taught.
Teacher monitors students' behavior.	No direct observation of student behavior. Teacher often works with other students or prepares for next lesson.
Feedback and discussion of students' behavior	No discussion of how well students worked together, other than general comments like "Nice job" or "Next time try working more quietly."

> **We have built up trust among us. No person is better than the other or has to do more work. The number of times I hear words of encouragement in my group is uncountable!**
>
> — Student

Before we go on to Chapter 2 and talk about why we think you should learn to use cooperative groups in your class, whatever grade or subject you teach, we have one final question:

When you put students into groups to work together, what do you do if they're not getting along well or not concentrating on the task?

Most teachers answer that question quickly: "Move them!" If that's your answer, too, the next chapter should prove interesting.

16

2

A Rationale For Using Cooperative Learning

"Why should I learn how to use cooperative groups in my classroom? Will they really make that much difference?"

W e know that you don't want to spend time learning a new strategy—especially one that takes a while to master—unless you can be sure that the effort you'll have to expend will be more than compensated for by the gains you and your students will receive.

What's great about cooperative learning is that both teachers *and* students benefit from its use. A cooperative classroom is a happier and more productive place for everybody. In fact, that sentence identifies the two kinds of gains teachers see in cooperative classes: social and academic.

Social Benefits of Cooperative Learning

It stands to reason that if students are regularly being taught how to work well with other students, they'll acquire social skills that will enable them to work—and play—comfortably with a wide range of people inside the classroom and out. Skills such as listening to others, taking turns, contributing ideas, explaining oneself clearly, encouraging others, and criticizing ideas and not people are important in almost all classroom and playground activities.

And these skills will be important later in life as well. No matter what kinds of work students eventually engage in, they will be expected to work with others. A study published by the Center for Public Resources in 1982 indicated that the main reason people lose their jobs is *not* that they don't have the skills for the job, but that they cannot get along with their co-workers.[1]

Social skills are equally important in personal relationships. Since our divorce rate is now about 50 percent, we know that many adults have difficulty working out the problems that arise in any marriage.

Sometimes teachers say, "Yes, I know students need to learn the skills of getting along well with others and working effectively in groups, but I don't have time to add social skills to my curriculum. It's already too crowded. And besides, teaching social skills really isn't my job. That's something students should be learning at home."

- We think it *is* the teacher's job to teach social skills, for two reasons: these skills are vitally important to students' future success, and they're not generally being learned—at home or anywhere else. And we believe that the investment of time in teaching social skills will more than be paid back in time gained, since students who know how to work together effectively are able to accomplish a great deal more than those who do not.

Let's look at why children aren't learning many social skills outside of school. Before the advent of television, computers, and Nintendo, children used to spend hours playing interactive games like hide-and-seek, kick-the-can, stickball, and Red Rover or board games like Sorry and Monopoly. They learned to wait for their turn, to compromise (or "do over"), to see other points of view, and to derive pleasure from contributing to the group's fun.

1. "Basic Skills in the Work Force," referred to in David W. Johnson and Roger T. Johnson, "Social Skills for Successful Group Work." *Educational Leadership.* December 1989/January 1990: p. 32.

Nowadays many students spend hours watching television or playing computer games. Especially in homes with one parent, or families in which both parents work outside the home, these electronic baby-sitters help keep children occupied when no one else is available.

The social activities in which children do participate tend to be managed by adults: organized sports instead of neighborhood games, programmed play dates, lessons, and after-school enrichment classes. In many communities even birthday parties are stage-managed.

The American penchant for fast food on the run and dinners in front of the television set has also reduced children's opportunities for social interaction with adults and other family members. Sometimes school is the only place where children really engage with other people for more than a few minutes at a time. For many children school has become the only place to learn social interaction skills.

> **I think working in groups is good, because everyone helps each other and no one is left out.**
> — Student

But Look at What Often Happens in Schools...

In the first chapter we asked you what you do if students are not working well together in a small group activity. And we said that when asked that question most teachers quickly respond, "Move them." Think about what that common practice teaches children:

- If I don't want to work with someone else, I don't have to.
- An easy way to get out of working with someone I don't like is to misbehave (or complain about that other student).
- Knowing how to work with other people isn't as important as knowing how to do my math (or social studies, or whatever).

Children know what we value by what we teach and what we reward. If we value the social skills necessary for learning and working effectively with others, we need to teach those social skills and provide incentives for students to use them.

Teachers who take the time to teach social skills see benefits in many school settings. Children begin to resolve playground disputes on their own. They're more willing to wait their turn. They help newcomers feel welcome to their class. They compliment each other. When a group is having difficulty making a decision they suggest compromises rather than insisting on their own way.

And parents will notice this cooperative behavior carrying over to the home, as well.

Of course, one of the main reasons teachers teach social skills is so that students will be able to do their academic work successfully in cooperative learning groups. This brings us to the second kind of positive outcome associated with cooperative learning: increased academic achievement.

"Learning material with the expectation that you will have to explain it to peers results in more frequent use of higher-level reasoning strategies than does learning material to pass a test. Orally explaining the material being studied results in higher achievement than does listening to the material being explained or reading it alone,"

David W. Johnson and Roger T. Johnson. "What to Say to the Parents of Gifted Students." *Our Cooperative Link,* April 1989. Page 1.

2. See David W. Johnson and Roger T. Johnson, *Cooperation and Competition: Theory and Research.* Edina, Minn.: Interaction Book Company, 1989.

Academic Gains From Cooperative Learning

A large number of research studies have demonstrated that cooperative learning is more effective than individualistic or competitive structures for increasing students' achievement *and* promoting their cognitive growth.[2]

There are several reasons for this. First is a concept cognitive psychologists call *oral rehearsal,* or thinking out loud. To learn, we need to talk about what we are thinking and to adjust our thinking as we hear ourselves saying things that don't quite make sense. Through talking, we discover what we know and what we don't yet understand.

A second reason for an increase in achievement is the increase in *time-on-task* that cooperative groups produce. Teachers who haven't yet used cooperative groups are often skeptical of this finding; teachers who *have* used them say that's one of the first things they notice. If you're in the skeptical group, think about how difficult it is to keep a classroom of children focused on a whole-class lesson or concentrated on individual work. In these settings it's easy for students to become distracted and let their attention wander. But in a group with one or two other students it's much harder to drift off without a group member noticing and pulling the wanderer back into the conversation or activity.

- Teachers particularly like the fact that cooperative groups get *them* out of the business of constantly trying to keep everybody on task.

Cooperative learning also promotes controversy. When students are regularly confronted with ideas and convictions different from their own, they learn to examine their own thinking and adjust it if necessary. Having to explain their thoughts to other group members helps them clarify their ideas and forces them to confront inconsistent or illogical reasoning. Listening to someone else explain his or her thoughts helps children see an issue from another person's perspective.

Another reason that cooperative learning stimulates achievement and cognitive growth also surprises some teachers: children often engage in more higher-order thinking (application, analysis, synthesis, and evaluation) in cooperative activities than they do in whole-class discussions—which tend to operate on the knowledge and comprehension level.

Finally, cooperative learning is effective because it promotes the development of children's *self-esteem.* As children experience success and support in their groups and as other children begin to ask for and need their contributions, they come to see themselves as competent learners who are valued by their peers.

Other Benefits of Cooperative Learning

In addition to these findings on improvement in academic achievement and social skills, research on cooperative learning has demonstrated a host of other positive outcomes, including promoting students' acceptance of differences, whether those differences result from handicaps or racial or ethnic backgrounds.

Another bonus that may appeal to you: children view teachers who use cooperative learning as more fair than teachers who do not, and they like those teachers better. They also like *school* better when their teacher uses cooperative learning groups.[3]

We hope we've given you enough justification for going ahead with cooperative learning groups in your classroom. In the next chapter we'll take you through the steps you need to follow to plan a cooperative lesson, and we'll suggest some topics and provide sample lesson plans.

3. David W. Johnson, Roger T. Johnson, and Edythe Johnson Holubec, *Cooperation in the Classroom* (Revised). Edina, Minn.: Interaction Book Company, 1988.

3

Getting Started

"How do I start using cooperative groups? I'm not sure where to begin, what to do first."

O
ur best advice is to *start simple*. Pick a lesson that's so easy you'd feel comfortable leaving it in your plans for a substitute. Or one that your students do so regularly they no longer need any instructions from you. Perhaps it's completing a worksheet of math problems, or writing a book report or story, or finding all the items in the room that begin with *b*.

Once you've decided the academic task, think about one social skill that would make cooperative accomplishment of that task easier for your students. With primary children it might be *taking turns*. Or simply *staying with your partner* until the job is done. Older children might need to concentrate on *listening* to their group mates or *contributing ideas*.

When you have selected the academic and social skills tasks, you're ready to make your lesson cooperative instead of individualistic or competitive. Let's look at each step of the process, starting with the four questions you'll need to answer *before* you introduce the cooperative lesson to your students:

- How big should the groups be?
- Which students should work together?
- Where will they work?
- What materials will they need?

Planning the Lesson

Group Size

You can experiment to see what size groups work best for you, but our advice is, Think small. The larger the group, the more skills children need to function well in it.

In fact, we encourage teachers of primary children to use pairs. By grade 3 or 4 children can work successfully in trios for certain tasks. Middle school students *can* work in quartets, but we'd advise you to hold off on groups of four for these students until they've had plenty of success working in pairs and trios. (Groups of four tend to separate into pairs, or into trios with a "wallflower," so you might as well plan for pairs or trios to start with.)

Assignment to Groups

Before you assign students to groups, think about what skills each group needs to have to complete the academic task. Will it be necessary for someone to be able to read? To write? To draw a picture or diagram? If certain skills are needed, be sure each group has at least one person with each of those skills.

For many tasks it's sufficient to put a relatively high achiever with a relatively low achiever, or to create a trio of "high," "middle," and "low." Think, too, of mixing up the children who are talkative, or boisterous, or withdrawn. Of course, you want to avoid putting two children together who tend to act out.

Remember that heterogeneous groups usually work best: it's the *differences* in group members that make cooperative learning effective. And don't think you have to assign students to work with children they like. Remember that one purpose of cooperative learning is to help students learn to work with everybody.

If the task is one that all your students can do, *eventually* you will be able to assign them to groups randomly. But while random grouping is easy to accomplish and clearly demonstrates to the children that you expect them to work well with everybody in the class, it's too risky for your *first* venture with cooperative learning. You're likely to end up with one or two ill-matched pairs or trios of students who don't work well together. Wait to use random assignment to groups until after your children have become more skilled at working in cooperative groups.

- When you're ready to use random grouping, the fastest way to randomly assign children to groups is to have them count off or pair up with the person next to them. You can also have fun experimenting with other random strategies, such as having students draw one-half of a math equation from a box and then find the person with the other half. (Or use sets of synonyms or homonyms, or matching shapes or colors, or vocabulary words and their definitions.)

Classroom Arrangement

Students working in groups need to be as close to their group mates—and as separated from other groups—as possible. Think about how best to accomplish this in your setting. Can students easily push their desks or chairs together? Can they find a quiet work space on a rug or in a corner or in the hall? How will you move them into their groups?

Materials

One way to create positive interdependence is to give students one set of materials (one worksheet, or one piece of paper and one pencil, or one set of math manipulatives, or one pair of scissors and one jar of paste). Decide whether that's a good strategy for the lesson you've chosen, or whether it would be better for each student to have a complete set of materials.

Carrying Out the Lesson

Now you're ready to try out your cooperative learning lesson with your students. Let's look at your next set of decisions:

"When students of different racial backgrounds work together toward a common goal, they gain liking and respect for one another. Cooperative learning also improves the social acceptance of mainstreamed academically handicapped students by their classmates... as well as increasing friendships among students in general."

Robert E. Slavin "Research on Cooperative Learning: Consensus and Controversy." *Educational Leadership,* Dec.1989/Jan.1990 Page 54.

- How should I introduce the idea of working cooperatively?
- How will I know if my students are staying on task and working well together?
- What should I do if I can see they're having difficulty?
- How can I evaluate the success of the groups?

We'll go into greater detail answering each of these questions in the next chapters, but for now, here's enough information and advice to get you started.

Setting the Stage

The first time you introduce cooperative learning, we encourage you to talk with your students about the importance of cooperation in their lives—and yours. You might begin by asking them to think about situations in which they've received help learning to do something or accomplishing some task. And you can describe ways in which you've benefited from the help of others, such as sharing a problem with a friend or working with other teachers to develop a curriculum.

- Be sure to keep the focus on *Two (or more) heads are better than one*, rather than *Many hands make light work*. While the latter aphorism is true, it's the former that expresses why we want children to be able to learn and work cooperatively.

Have your students brainstorm a list of key rules for working together successfully, such as No put-downs; Use quiet voices; Help each other; and Get the job done. The list can be posted and added to as students gain more experience working in groups.

Describing the Tasks

It's important for students to learn that a cooperative learning activity always has *two* different tasks, an *academic* task and a *social skills* task. And it's especially important for them to know that you value their success at learning social skills just as much as you value their academic achievement. So, always begin a cooperative learning lesson by describing what students need to do to be successful at both tasks.

For older children you can actually use the words *academic* and *social skills*: "Your *academic* task is to solve all the word problems on this page and be prepared to explain both *how* your group solved each problem and *why* it chose a particular strategy. I should be able to call on anyone in your group to defend the group's decisions. Your *social skills* task is to contribute your ideas to the group's discussion of each problem. When I come around, I will be looking for each person in your group to be contributing ideas."

For young children you might say simply, "Your pair has *two* jobs. One job is to find six objects in the room that begin with the sound of your group's letter. Each time you find an object that you *both* agree starts with the sound of your letter, you will tape one of your group's paper letters to the object, so we'll all know which ones you found. Your other job is to remember to *take turns* taping the letters. As I watch each group working, I'll be listening to see if you check with your partner to be sure you both agree that an object starts with the sound of your letter, and I'll be looking to see if you take turns taping the letters."

Moving Students Into Groups

Now it's time for you to tell your students which groups they are in and to give them instructions for moving quickly and quietly into their groups. Before you actually give out the group assignments, however, assure your students that eventually they will have an opportunity to work with everyone in the room.

Monitoring Your Students' Interaction

Once your students are working on their tasks, it's time for you to monitor their behavior. You'll do this by walking around to each group, watching them work for a few minutes, and jotting down information about their interactions.

The simplest way to collect information is to make a chart (*see Charts A and B*). List the names of the students in each group down the left side and put the social skill(s) you're looking for across the top. We encourage you to start with just one social skill, but soon you'll probably find yourself identifying two for your students to work on, such as listening and encouraging or giving compliments and checking for understanding.

As you watch a group, put a check in the box next to a student's name each time he or she uses the skill. You can also jot down specific student comments and your own observations—about that skill or the academic task or anything else you'll want to remember later.

After you've finished watching a group, you may want to give them

Social Skills

Group A		
Group B		
Group C		

Chart A

Social Skills

	CONTRIB-UTING IDEAS	ENCOUR-AGING OTHERS	
Group A			
John	✓✓✓	✓	"Here's how we do this"
Marie	✓✓✓	✓✓	"Bob, what do you think?"
Bob	✓		
Group B			
Sally	✓✓		
Phil	✓	✓✓	"That's a great idea!"
John H.	✓✓		
Group C			
Xavier	✓✓✓		
Jeanne	✓	✓	
Michael	✓		

Chart B

27

feedback right then, rather than waiting until the end of the lesson. Show them your chart and describe what you learned: "While I was watching, Johnny contributed his ideas six times, and Susie and Joan each contributed ideas twice. I also heard Joan say, 'Wait, I have another idea of how we could do this,' and Susie and Johnny both said, 'Great, what is it?' So I know you're helping each other contribute ideas."

Concentrate on positive feedback. If one student has no or very few checks for a social skill, don't let that situation become the student's problem; it's the group's problem. "While I was watching, Paul didn't say much. How could you help him feel comfortable contributing his ideas?"

> **When I had a problem on one of my worksheets, no one said, "Oh, come on, that's so easy," or , "You're stupid." They just looked at it, read it, and then explained how they figured it out.**
> — Student

Intervening When Necessary

If you observe students having trouble, stop them and help them figure out how to solve their problem ("Can you think of a way you could share these materials?" "How could you get the information you need?") or teach them the skill they need to proceed ("When someone's not understanding you, often it helps to explain your idea in a different way or to give a different example." "If you want to know if Carol understands how to do this, ask her to show you how she would solve the problem.").

Whenever you can, turn the problem back to the students so that they develop skill at problem solving and so that they can become more confident in their own abilities and less dependent on you. You may want to make a rule that students may raise their hands and ask for your help only after they've asked each of their group members. After your students have become accustomed to group work, you may even amend the rule to require checking with another group before calling on you.

If you see several students having the same difficulty, you may decide to stop the whole class and teach everyone how to handle that problem ("It looks as if a lot of people are having trouble knowing when to multiply first. Let's review our process.") or engage in whole-class problem solving ("I see several groups in which one person is doing most of the talking and the other group members are just copying down answers. How could your group make sure that doesn't happen?").

If you notice that most students are getting their academic task done but ignoring the social skills task, you may decide to let everyone finish and then talk with the whole class about what you observed.

Evaluating the Groups' Work

Be sure to plan for time at the end of the lesson when you and the students can evaluate their work. Because cooperative groups always have two kinds of tasks, you will need to have two kinds of evaluations.

You can evaluate students' success with the academic task immediately— through checking their work, asking them questions, or having them hand it in—or later, by giving a test on another day or asking for a demonstration of what they have learned.

- If you said you would check to see if each person in the groups understood and could defend the group's work, be sure to call on several children in different groups so that they realize they really are being held accountable for their own and their group mates' learning.

The evaluation of your students' use of social skills comes from two sources: the information you collected as you watched the groups work; and the students' assessment of their own and their group's effectiveness.

If you've given individual groups feedback as you watched them work, you can make some general encouraging statements to the whole class at the end, such as "I noticed good listening going on in just about every group" or "I saw many people contributing their ideas to the discussion," and you can repeat some of the appropriate comments you overheard.

Then turn the evaluation over to the students. Ask them to say one thing their partner(s) did to help the group be successful. You can also ask them to identify something they themselves did to contribute to their group.

And finally, ask students to think about what they could do better next time. If most of your students name the same or similar social skills (such as "listen better" and "not interrupt") you may decide to make that skill the focus of your next cooperative learning lesson. If your groups have different needs (and if your students are able to write well enough), you can ask each group to fill out a form like *Chart C*.

> **This time we were good at** _____
> _____
> _____
>
> **Next time we will work on** _____
> _____
> _____
>
> **Signed:** _____
> _____
> _____
>
> **Date:** _____

Chart C

Eventually you won't have to take time after each lesson to have students evaluate their group process. But it's important to spend as much time as necessary focusing on acquiring good group skills when students are first learning to work in cooperative groups.

Looking Back

Congratulations! You've tried your first cooperative learning lesson. What went well? Were there any surprises? Would you do anything differently another time?

In the next three chapters we'll help you move from "basic" to "intermediate" cooperative learning. And we'll try to anticipate problems you may have and help you solve them.

Our Best Advice

As you explore using cooperative learing groups, don't rush. Take your time with this new strategy. Use a variety of cooperative group activities in just one curriculum area for a while until you and your students feel comfortable and secure.

And above all, enjoy your accomplishments.

4

Creating Positive Interdependence and Individual Accountability

"When my students are working in groups, how can I be sure that no one person dominates and that *all* kids do their work?"

Research on cooperative learning makes it clear that cooperative groups are effective in promoting students' achievement only when the groups are structured so that kids are *both* **interdependent** *and* **individually accountable**. Your students truly have to believe We sink or swim together and There's no hitchhiking in our groups.

Positive Interdependence

Let's look at several strategies for creating positive interdependence, some of which rely on the structure of the academic and social skills tasks you assign while others make use of incentives and rewards.

Materials

A simple way to get students to work together is to provide only one set of materials—one answer sheet or one set of lab equipment or one list of questions or one reference book. Sometimes you'll choose to instruct students to take turns with the materials, and sometimes it will make more sense to give each of them different roles or tasks as they work with that one set of materials.

Roles

You can assign a variety of **roles** to group members. Having a role to play not only helps keep students on task; it also allows each student to shine in an area of special strength or to get practice in a skill.

> **It feels good when someone says "You're doing a good job." We encourage each other.**
>
> — Student

For example, if groups of three are going to work together to answer the questions in a weekly student newspaper, one student in each trio could be the reader, who reads each question to the group. One could be the writer and write down the group's answers. The third student could be the reporter, who reads an answer to the whole class when called upon and is prepared to discuss the group's reasons for choosing that answer.

Different academic tasks call for different roles. Sometimes groups will need a **graph-maker** or **illustrator** to accomplish their task. Some math activities call for a **counter** or **problem-solver.** Tasks involving materials may require a **materials handler.** If all students are reasonably able to perform each role, you can rotate the roles until all have had a chance to be successful in them.

If you have severely limited youngsters, you can create academic roles that these students can manage and that allow them to contribute to the group's functioning. For example, a child who cannot write may be proficient at drawing and could be asked to draw a diagram or a picture that represents the group's best thinking. But don't make such adjustments too quickly. Often a youngster who has difficulty writing when alone will blossom in a small group with partners who are encouraging and helpful.

Assigning social skills roles also promotes positive interdependence. A student can be a group's official **encourager**, making sure everyone has a chance to contribute ideas and is complimented for those contributions. Or a group may need a **time-keeper** to help the group stay on task and finish its job, or a **checker** to make sure everyone understands the material.

You can mix academic and social skills roles in one lesson. In fact, many three-person assignments call for a **reader**, **recorder**, and **encourager**.

Tasks

You can make students interdependent by giving each group member a part of the group's task to complete. For example, after agreeing on a topic of mutual interest, a group of students could take turns writing sentences for a paragraph. Or one might do the first step in a lab procedure, another the second, another the third, while the fourth writes up the results. (Be sure to build in individual accountability—described later in this chapter—so that students are interested in the total result rather than just their parts.)

Group Spirit

If you plan to keep students together for several days or weeks, think about giving them some time during their first meeting together to develop a sense of group identity. They can choose a group name, select a group color, develop a group emblem, even write a group cheer. If your classroom arrangement permits, groups can chose their own spot for working and decorate it with a poster or sign identifying their favorite books or foods or sports.

Jigsaw

A complex strategy for creating interdependence is called the jigsaw. We like this process, especially for social studies topics, but we warn you that it takes time to do well, and it isn't appropriate for primary students.

To conduct a jigsaw, first divide up a set of information. For example, if fifth graders are studying Abraham Lincoln, you would divide the information they are going to learn into categories, such as Lincoln's childhood and education; his activities as a lawyer and writer; his campaign for the presidency; and his role in the Civil War. After you put students into "home groups" of four, assign each student in a group to be responsible for a different set of information.

Tell the students that they are to learn their information and prepare themselves to teach it to their group mates. We encourage you to provide study questions to guide their learning, and to ask them to write out their answers to these questions before they participate in the next step. (This part of the jigsaw can be done in class or as a homework assignment.)

The next step is to bring students together into "expert groups." All the students who are becoming "experts" about Lincoln's childhood and education get together, as do all the students who are studying his early career, and so on. If your expert groups are too big (six or more students), divide them into two groups or more.

Students in their expert groups first review what they have learned and help each other clear up any confusion. Next they share what they have written and come to an agreement on what is important to teach. Finally, they plan how they will teach their home groups this material. You have a key role to play here. As you monitor the groups' discussions, you can give pointers on how to teach, such as using charts or other visuals to help convey information.

Finally the experts return to their home groups and take turns teaching their group mates the material they have learned. The study questions you provided can become the test given to all students to see if they have learned the material.

> **I learned that cooperation is essential in order to have a good and responsible group. Listening is very important. Another good quality to have is to be able to explain things and be very patient. When you help a person understand, it makes you feel really good.**
>
> — Student

Rewards

One popular strategy (popular with children, that is) for fostering interdependence is giving rewards when a group accomplishes its goal or every member reaches a set criterion. Stickers, bonus points, privileges such as computer time or independent reading time, snacks, a party—whatever appeals to your students and you can be used as a reward.

Rewards are particularly appropriate when it's easy to quantify students' success, such as counting the number of vocabulary or spelling words learned, math problems solved correctly, or historical facts memorized correctly.

For example, if your students are helping each other learn new vocabulary words, put them into groups of three and assign four words to each student to teach to his or her group mates. When the groups are tested on all twelve words, if every member of a group gets at least ten words right, award each student in that group two bonus points. If everyone gets eleven words right, give three bonus points. If everyone gets them all correct, four bonus points.

Spelling pairs can be given a pretest on Monday. Each pair then sets its own goal for Friday's test. Pairs help each other study their words, and if both members of the pair reach their goal, each child gets a sticker.

Some teachers give a sticker to each group member if everyone in the group brings in completed homework. You can give a reward to the whole class— perhaps a party on a Friday — if all groups bring in their homework all week.

34

Group Grades

A controversial method of structuring group interdependence is giving a single grade to the group. (Parents of "gifted" children sometimes object to this strategy because they think their own children are being held back or "punished" by having their grade affected by the work of less capable children.) Group grades are most appropriate when it's clear that all students have contributed to a group product.

One such situation could be a group presentation. For example, for Black History Month students could be put into groups to research the life of an African American they admire. Each group could prepare a presentation to the class on its chosen person, with one group member creating and displaying a poster, one delivering an oral presentation, and one writing a short autobiography to be added to the class library. Or the group could write and present a skit in which all take part.

- One problem you may have when giving group grades is a student who simply will not do his or her work, no matter how much pressure the group applies. If that happens, intervene to support the other groups members in their efforts to include the recalcitrant student. Ultimately you may decide to remove the student from the group, tell him or her to work on the assignment alone, and grade the remaining pair or trio on their joint efforts.

Another way teachers award group grades is by collecting just one paper from a group. For example, if students have been discussing and then writing answers to study questions or working math problems together, you can select one paper at random from each group and grade just that paper. (A teacher we know shuffles them behind her back and then pulls one out.) Not only does this strategy encourage students to be sure everyone's answers are complete and accurate, but it also cuts down on the number of papers you have to read.

Group Product

Sometimes it makes sense for a group to create a single product, such as a poem, a set of rules for operating the computer, or a letter to a politician. These activities can be designed specifically to help groups learn the skill of coming to consensus.

Our Best Advice

We encourage you to use as many strategies for promoting positive interdependence as possible within one lesson. Roles are particularly easy to combine with other strategies, and they serve as a constant reminder to students that each group member has an important contribution to make to the group's success.

*"Cooperation does not work under all conditions. It is only in certain instances that group efforts may be expected to be more productive than individual efforts. These conditions are: 1. Clearly perceived **positive interdependence** that promotes personal responsibility to achieve the group's goals...2. Considerable **face-to-face interaction** in which participants provide each other with help and assistance, exchange needed resources, provide each other with helpful feedback, challenge each other's reasoning, advocate the exertion of effort to achieve the group's goals, are open to each other's influence, act in trusting and trustworthy ways, demonstrate high achievement motivation, and exhibit low anxiety and stress...3. Frequent use of relevant **interpersonal and small group skills**, with frequent and regular **group processing** to improve the group's future effectiveness,"*

David W. Johnson and Roger T. Johnson. *Cooperation and Competition: Theory and Research.* Edina, Minn. : Interaction Book Company, 1989. Page 173. [Emphasis added]

Individual Accountability

While maintaining individual accountability in cooperative learning groups is not difficult, it can't be left to chance. Just as you'll need to think about how you're promoting positive interdependence in each cooperative lesson, you'll also need to build in some strategy for making sure no students are hitchhiking and all are learning the material. Here are several that are easy to use.

Signatures

One way to remind students that they are accountable for their group's work is to have them sign their names to any group product. Requiring signatures won't guarantee that everyone participates, but it does tell students that you expect them to take responsibility for their behavior in their group.

Whenever you ask students to sign a paper, be sure you explain clearly just what it is that their signature represents. You could say, for example, "When you sign your name, you are saying that you agree with your group's answers and that you can explain those answers if I call on you." Or "Your signature means that you contributed your ideas to the discussion, you support your group's decision, and you will abide by it."

Sampling

Another way to show students that they are each accountable is to call on individual students at random to discuss some part of their group's work. For example, after groups have solved math story problems, ask the oldest (or youngest, or tallest) student in each group to come to the board and work a particular problem. (You can also ask students to count off within their group and then invite "All the No. 3s to the board," and so on.)

Of course, you don't have to bring students up to the blackboard to hold them accountable. A quick trip around the room, calling on one student from each group to share an idea or answer allows you to see if most are understanding the work and makes it clear to the students that you expect them to learn the material. In fact, you don't even have to call on one student from each group, provided you call on each of them over time so that all expect to be held accountable.

Testing

Individual accountability can also be maintained through regular quizzes and tests. There's no need to follow every group activity by some kind of individual assessment, but regular testing of each student's understanding of material is important—both to keep students aware of their own responsibility to learn and to inform you of how much they are actually learning.

Many teachers use cooperative learning groups to help students prepare for weekly spelling or vocabulary or math tests. While this use of cooperative groups is fine, we encourage you also to think of cooperative groups as ends in themselves—as activities that foster the development of social skills, deep comprehension of academic material, and higher-order thinking. If you adopt this second point of view, your tests will become vehicles for assessing those skills, comprehension, and thinking, rather than the focus of classroom instruction.

Checkpoints

When students are working on a long-term project in their group, such as the presentations for Black History Month described above, you can help them develop organizational skills and hold them accountable for their work by building in checkpoints. These are dates when each student must come to you with a certain portion of the task completed.

Journals

Cooperative learning journals can also be used to foster self-awareness and accountability. You can ask your students to write in their journals after each cooperative lesson, once a day, or once a week. Invite them to reflect on a variety of questions, such as "What have I contributed to my group?" or "What am I learning about working with others?" or "What skill should I work on to be a better group member?"

You can use the journals to engage in a written dialogue with your students about their successes and their progress toward greater success. This is a particularly good way to give positive feedback and encouragement to students who are having difficulty learning to cooperate.

More Advice

As with positive interdependence, the more ways you can foster individual accountability, the better. Your students need to become convinced that cooperative groups will help them learn, not take the place of their learning. Fortunately, since cooperative groups *do* make it easier for students to be successful, youngsters in such groups quickly discover that they don't need to avoid doing their schoolwork in order to avoid failure. Once you've made cooperative learning an integral part of your classroom, we predict you'll see a dramatic increase in both the amount and quality of individual student work.

"There is wide agreement among reviewers of the cooperative learning literature that cooperative methods can and usually do have a positive effect on student achievement. Further, there is almost as strong a consensus that the achievement effects...depend on two essential features....One of these features is **group goals,** *or positive interdependence....The second essential feature is* **individual accountability."**

Robert E. Slavin. "Research on Cooperative Learning: Consensus and Controversy." *Educational Leadership,* Dec.1989/Jan.1990. Page 52. [Emphasis in original]

5

Teaching Social Skills

"What social skills will my students need to be successful in cooperative learning groups? How can I teach those skills?"

Y our students will need help learning to work with others. Most children (like most adults) don't have well-developed social skills, so you'll have to teach them those skills, just as you teach them to write or to multiply or to conduct scientific experiments.

We have divided social skills into three kinds: Basic Group Skills, Functioning Skills, and Higher-Order Thinking Skills. The lists below contain examples of the kinds of skills we think are essential. We're sure you'll think of others.

Basic Group Skills are those bottom-line skills without which a group can't get anything done:

- getting into your group quietly and quickly
- bringing necessary materials with you
- staying with your group until the task is done
- talking in quiet voices
- listening to your partner(s)
- calling your partner(s) by name
- knowing your task(s)

Functioning Skills enable group members to work together effectively so that the group can accomplish its task and each member can learn the material. Most functioning skills can be learned to some degree by all elementary and middle school students:

- taking turns
- contributing your ideas
- supporting your point with evidence*
- asking for help when you need it
- encouraging others to contribute
- complimenting others' contributions
- checking for understanding
- keeping the group focused on the task

* This is a difficult skill for elementary students, but it's essential for them to learn it.

Higher-Order Thinking Skills deepen group members' understanding of the material being learned and the points of view of other students. While young children can learn some of these skills, others are appropriate only for students in grades 4 through 8 who have developed good Functioning Skills:

- asking for clarification

"Systematic and frequent use of small-group procedures has a profound positive effect upon the classroom climate; the classroom becomes a community of learners, actively working together to enhance each person's...knowledge, proficiency, and enjoyment."

Neil Davidson. "Introduction and Overview." *Cooperative Learning in Mathematics.* N. Davidson, ed. N.Y.: Addison-Wesley, 1990.

- providing clarification
- building on another's ideas
- paraphrasing another's idea to show you understand it
- analyzing your group's process
- coming to consensus
- synthesizing several ideas
- evaluating the group's work
- criticizing an idea, not the person who presented it

Choosing a Focus

Don't be overwhelmed by the number of skills listed. You don't have to teach your students *all* these skills. In fact, we encourage teachers in primary grades to focus on just three or four skills for the entire school year. Intermediate and middle school teachers may work on more skills during a school year, but never more than two or three at a time, and never moving so fast that students can't experience success.

When you begin to teach social skills, we advise starting with something simple from the Basic Group Skills. For the lower grades "getting into your group quickly and quietly" is a good idea. For older children perhaps "using quiet voices" or "calling your group members by name" will be more appropriate. (This last skill is particularly difficult—and important—for middle school students.)

Don't be afraid to teach "baby" skills to older students. If you find that your students need to learn a skill you would have expected them to master when they were much younger, go ahead and teach it to them again.

> **If somebody in your cooperative group doesn't know how to behave, the good person can show them how to behave. The bad kids can watch and learn how to behave. It works!**
>
> — Student

Teaching a Social Skill

We recommend using the following six-step process whenever you teach a social skill. The amount of time you spend on each step will depend on the complexity of the skill.

1. Define the skill in terms students can understand. Be as explicit as possible.

- "When I say, 'Get into your groups quickly and quietly,' I mean that you should pick up the materials you will need and go directly to your work spot without any talking."

41

2. Help students see the need for the skill. A quick way to do this is to describe what happens when the skill isn't used:

- "Yesterday you spent almost five minutes getting into your groups and getting ready for work. That cut short your working time, and many of you had to rush to finish the assignment."

For variety—and fun—set up a role play that shows what happens when a particular skill isn't used. Students will especially enjoy it if you do the role play with another teacher, an administrator, or an aide, but if another adult isn't available, use one or two of your students to role-play with you. Be sure to talk with them ahead of time and be very clear about just what they are to do.

You can also ask students to talk with you about the need for a skill:

- "Why do you suppose you ran out of time to finish your task yesterday? What happened to cut short your working time?"

3. Have students describe the skill. Record their description and keep it in view. A T-chart, (*see Charts D, E and F*) can be drawn on big easel pads and either left standing on the easel where everyone can see it or pinned to a bulletin board or taped to the end of the blackboard. If you don't have access to easel pads, use news-print, construction paper, or oak tag.

- "Let's describe what it looks like when you are getting into your working spot quickly and quietly....And now tell me what it sounds like when you are getting into your working spot quickly and quietly."

4. Have students practice the skill.

- "Let's practice getting into our working spots. I'm going to watch the clock and see how quickly you can do it this time."

5. Discuss and reinforce students' efforts.

- "That time you took just twenty-five seconds.

T-Chart

LOOKS LIKE	SOUNDS LIKE

Chart D

Getting into our groups quickly and quietly	
LOOKS LIKE	SOUNDS LIKE
• lips closed • walking directly to working spot • no running! • lifting chairs so they don't scrape the floor • carrying work materials on first trip (no returning to seat for something you forgot)	• QUIET! • tiptoeing feet

Chart E   42

That's a big improvement! In fact, I think you may have been concentrating on speed so much that you forgot to be as quiet as possible. Does anyone have an idea about how we could eliminate the noise of the chairs scraping the floor?"

6. Have students practice the skill as often as needed. Return to a skill whenever students seem to be forgetting to use it.

- "We haven't practiced getting into our work groups quickly and quietly for a while, and I've noticed that we're starting to take longer and get noisy again. Let's take a few minutes to look over our T-chart and talk about what we said it would look like and sound like when we are getting into our working spots....OK, now let's see how quickly and quietly we can do it."

Evaluating and Reinforcing Social Skills Use

Our students know what we value by what we reinforce. Always evaluate and reinforce your students' use of the social skill(s) you have asked for. We'll talk about ways to evaluate group work in the next chapter, but for now, think of simple ways to let a group know that they're doing well. For example, putting a star on a group's paper as you circulate works wonders, even for older students.

Moving Beyond the Basics

While it's important to start with the Basic Group Skills and make sure your students can perform them, cooperative learning groups are most effective when students use Functioning Skills and—where appropriate—Higher-Order Thinking Skills.

To choose one or more of the advanced social skills, look at the academic task and see what skill will help the group achieve its goal. For example, if a group is writing a paragraph together, "expressing support and acceptance of others' ideas" would be important. If your students are studying for a test, you could ask them to practice "seeking clever ways to remember important ideas." If a group is solving math story problems, "checking for understanding" is a crucial skill to use.

Sometimes the skill you choose will grow out of your observation of the students' interactions. For example, you may notice that students are interrupting each other and not letting anyone develop a complete thought. That's

T-Chart

LISTENING	
LOOKS LIKE	SOUNDS LIKE
• eye contact	• quiet
• nodding	• "Um." "OK"
• leaning toward speaker	• "Are you saying...?"
• one person Talking	

Chart F

the time to teach a lesson on listening, or for older students you might select "paraphrasing to show you understand an idea."

Every class has its own dynamic, and some classes take longer than others to learn certain skills. You may find that with one class you have to work on a particular skill (like "using quiet voices") all year long while you are simultaneously teaching a variety of Functioning and Higher-Order Thinking Skills.

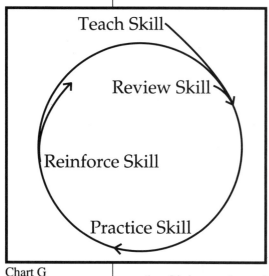

Chart G

- Speaking of the skill "using quiet voices," sometimes you'll get better results by asking for "eighteen-inch" or "fifty-centimeter" voices. You can even give your students a fifty-centimeter-long strip of paper to remind them how far their voices should carry.

Once your students become used to working in cooperative groups, you may decide to let individual groups pick their own social skill to practice, since different groups are likely to have different needs. Giving students the chance to select their own skill helps build commitment to the process of acquiring social skills.

Ensuring Success

Label Ladder

The more opportunities students have to practice a skill, the more adept they will become at using it. So—although teachers in grades 4 through 8 may teach several social skills during the course of a year—it's important to return regularly to earlier skills and provide more practice.

Think of learning social skills as a circular process: you never really stop teaching a skill until its use has become automatic (*see Chart G*).

Sometimes an individual student will need private coaching on a particular skill. Go ahead and provide it, and be sure to notice and reinforce his or her improvement in use of the skill.

Use quiet voices

Call partner by name

Say encouraging words

Check for understanding

Chart H

Providing Visual Reminders

We encourage you to provide as many visual aids as you can think of when you're teaching social skills. For example, use oak-tag strips to make a label for each skill and hang the label for the skill

44

being practiced in a prominent spot. You can make small holes in the labels and make a "label ladder," adding new skills as you teach them.

Whenever you begin a cooperative learning lesson, you can use the ladder for a quick review of skills already learned (*see Chart H*). Clip on a large star or arrow or other marker to indicate the particular focus of that day's lesson.

T-charts are essential for recording and posting students' own descriptions of a skill. If you have an easel for your T-charts, you can flip through the pad and find the chart for a previously taught skill that needs reinforcement. If you don't have an easel, you can pin or tape new charts on top of the old ones. When you need a particular chart, roll up the ones on top of it and fasten them with paper clips to keep them out of the way while you review the pertinent T-chart.

Chart I

For a skill like "encouraging," or "praising other's contributions," students have fun writing as many examples as they can think of on a roll of adding machine tape, which you can then hang up along a wall or across the top of the blackboard (*see Chart I*).

Or you can have each group make a poster containing all the encouraging words and phrases its members like to hear. Hang that poster in their working spot so that the group—and you—can refer too it.

You may decide your students need a poster of things that are *not* done or said. For example, most upper elementary and middle school youngsters need to learn the social skill "no put-downs." Go ahead and have them make a list of all the put-downs they can think of and then draw a wide red line diagonally through the list— the international symbol for "no." This poster can hang next to one that lists the class's favorite words of encouragement (*see Chart J*).

Our Best Advice

You will get lots of mileage out of teaching your students two social skills that you might not think are important: "using each other's names" and "encouraging your partner(s)." Students' use of these two skills quickly makes their cooperative groups places they want to be, where they feel valued and where they can enjoy learning.

We predict that you'll also notice these skills carried over into other settings—that you'll overhear students saying, "Good job, Tiffany!" on the playground or, "You can do it, Richard!" in a computer lab. Parents are likely to tell you that they notice a similar change at home, too.

Chart J

6

Monitoring And Evaluating Student Interaction

"How do I know if students are using social skills successfully? How can I possibly observe all the groups for more than a few seconds if an activity lasts less than twenty minutes?"

Progress Chart

Skill: _____

Students				
Group:				
Group:				
Group:				

Chart K

Skill: *Encouraging*

Students	Mon.	Tues.	Wed.	Thurs.
Group: #1 Leo	✔	✔✔✔	✔✔✔	✔✔✔
Jose	✔✔	✔	✔✔✔	✔✔✔
Sandy	✔	✔	✔✔✔	✔✔✔
Maria		✔	✔	✔✔
Group: #2 Alex	✔	✔	✔✔✔	✔✔✔
Jennifer	✔✔	✔✔✔	✔✔	✔✔✔
Juan	✔	✔	✔✔✔	✔✔✔
Group: #3 Emma	✔	✔✔	✔✔✔	✔✔✔
Shari		✔✔	✔✔✔	✔✔

Chart L   48

While most teachers accept the importance of checking on groups to see if students are actually using the social skills(s) being taught and are getting their academic task done effectively, some worry that monitoring group work will be a difficult job—that it will result in a lot of paperwork and record keeping or that it will be impossible to do in a large class.

While we urge you always to monitor your students' interactions and to provide them with feedback regularly, we think there are several ways you can do this—even in a large class—without creating mountains of work for yourself.

Developing a Form for Data Collection

In Chapter 3 we showed you a simple form you can use to collect data on students' use of social skills. That form works well for monitoring students in a one-time activity, and you can discard the sheets after you have shared them with the students. (Since you will have data for more than one group on each sheet, cover the data you have collected for other groups while you're giving feedback to a particular group. That way you won't promote competition among groups.)

You will also want to keep students in the same groups for a period of time so that they will have an opportunity to learn to work well together. Perhaps you've assigned spelling partners who will stay together for a month or longer, or social studies groups that will work together on a project for two to three weeks, or math groups that work together daily until a chapter is finished. It's important to show these students their progress in learning social skills during the life of a group.

Here is a data-gathering form that provides room to keep track of students' behavior for several days (*see Charts K and L*). If you use a different color pen for each day, it will be even easier for your students to see their progress.

To keep track of these sheets while the groups last, we recommend that you use a clipboard. The firm backing allows you to write notes easily while walking around the room, and the clip lets you keep your sheets safely in place. A loose-leaf notebook also works well, but it's a little more awkward to write in when you're standing up.

Sharing the Data You Collect

The easiest way to give feedback is to watch each group for a few minutes and then show the members what you've observed by sharing the data you gathered.

- As we indicated in Chapter 3, we encourage you to be *descriptive*, rather than *evaluative*, when you show students the data. For example, "I saw William contribute ideas once and make encouraging remarks five times," rather than "William did a good job of encouraging, but he needs to work on contributing ideas." You can then ask students for their reaction to the data, which allows them to make their own analyses.

Pace yourself. If you have eight groups of three working on a twenty-five-minute task, expect to spend about two to three minutes watching a group and collecting data, and one to two minutes showing your data and asking group members for their reactions. If you have fourteen pairs working on a ten-minute task, you can't get around to every group, so pick five key groups and watch each for a minute and allow them to react to your feedback sheet for about a minute.

Getting Students Involved in Evaluating Their Own Behavior

What happens if you can't get around to every group in a particular lesson? First of all, don't worry about it. If you use cooperative groups regularly, and your students know that they will be observed frequently, it won't matter if sometimes they don't get direct feedback from you.

Second, while you are an important source of information for your students about their behavior, you're not the only source. (Yes, colleagues, aides, and visitors can all be enlisted to gather data, and if you have access to other adults, we encourage you to use them. But many teachers don't regularly have other adults in their classrooms.) We're talking about getting your students to help monitor and evaluate their own performance in their groups. Not only does this ease your burden, but it also enables students to take responsibility for their own behavior.

There are two ways you can get students to monitor and evaluate their use of social skills. You can ask students to take time at the end of a lesson to reflect back on their participation in the group activity and decide what they did well and what they would like to improve. And you can actually use students as observers.

Student Self-Monitoring

Students at any age can engage in self-monitoring. Pairs of kindergarten students can be asked to check a smiling face or a sad face for whatever social skills(s) they are working on. Be sure to ask students to discuss their behavior and come to agreement before checking any faces (*see Chart M*).

Older students can have a similar form, with words such as *always*, *most of the time*, *sometimes*, *not very much* to check instead of faces. (*see Chart N and O*). You can have students fill out the group version of this sheet on their own and then compare their answers with their group mates, or ask the groups to discuss their interactions and come to agreement among themselves before filling out one form for the group. Each member then signs the form to indicate his or her agreement with the group's evaluation.

We have included an individual version of this form, because sometimes you may decide to have students rate their own performance. This may be a private evaluation, just between you and each student, or you may ask students

Today we:

Took turns:_____ _____

Helped each other: _____ _____

Signed: _____

_____

Chart M

Group:_____ Date:_____
1. We each contributed our ideas
often _____ sometimes_____ not very often_____
2. We listened to each other
often _____ sometimes_____ not very often_____
3. We encouraged each other
often _____ sometimes_____ not very often_____
4. We built on each others ideas
often _____ sometimes_____ not very often_____

Chart N

Name:_____ Date:_____
1. I contributed my ideas
often _____ sometimes_____ not very often_____
2. I listened to my partners
often _____ sometimes_____ not very often_____
3. I encouraged my partners
often _____ sometimes_____ not very often_____
4. I built on my partners ideas
often _____ sometimes_____ not very often_____

Chart O

to share their self-evaluation with their group members and ask for their partners' feedback. (Obviously you wouldn't ask students to share their self-evaluations with their groups until you were certain the groups are genuinely supportive of each group member.)

Another strategy for self-monitoring is to ask students to discuss their group's interactions and agree to a rating. For example, groups could choose from the following:

Super Group: We did everything we were supposed to do and we did it well.

Great Group: We did just about everything we were supposed to do, but we need to work a little harder at _____.

Good Group: We did some things well, but we had a real problem with _____.

If necessary, you can have a category for groups which are not yet able to work together at all:

Fair Group: We didn't get much done because we had such a problem with _____.

To avoid a superficial discussion ("I think we were super. Do you agree?") tell students to give specific reasons to support the rating they choose. You can make a quick trip around the room, asking each group to announce its rating and give the justification, or you can walk among the groups and check their ratings privately.

As we suggested in Chapter 3, another strategy for self-monitoring is to ask each student to write something he or she did particularly well and identify a skill to work on next time. Or the group can come to agreement on what it did well and what it would like to work on next time. One group member writes down the group's decision, and all members sign it.

It isn't necessary to have students fill out a form after each cooperative learning activity. For variety, sometimes just have them discuss their use of the particular social skill(s) you were focusing on that day. A real morale booster is to have each student talk directly to the other members of the group, using each person's name and describing something she or he did that helped the group: "Roy, I really liked it when you explained how to solve that problem so that I could understand it, and Joanne, I felt good when you said, "Go ahead, you can do it!' "

You can also pass out three-by-five-inch cards to each student and ask him or her to write a card to each group member describing what that person did to help the group. We encourage you to have the students show you their cards first (Don't worry: this takes just a few seconds), so that you can be sure they haven't written something negative, and so that you can ask them to be more specific if they write something general like "Maria, you were very helpful today."

Quick Check

When you run out of time, don't ignore the importance of asking students to evaluate their use of social skills. Instead, ask for a quick check: "Thumbs up if your group worked well today. Thumbs down if you're not happy with your group's work today. Thumbs to the side if you have mixed feelings." While you will get just a general impression of the groups' evaluations of their interactions, you will have reminded them that you are always interested in how they work together, not just in what they accomplish.

Using Student Observers

If you teach grades 3 through 8, you can enlist student help in conducting observations of groups as soon as your students are used to working together. Students in the primary grades usually have difficulty observing and recording behavior, but if you teach in those grades and think your students can handle the task, go ahead and try.

Asking two students each to observe two groups frees you up to spend more time with the remaining groups. Equally important, using students as observers provides them with the opportunity to learn more about social skills and to improve their own use of them.

When students are collecting data, it's usually a good idea to have them look for just one skill that's relatively easy to observe, such as "encouraging participation," "contributing ideas," or "everyone does his or her job" (if roles have been assigned).

It's important to meet with the students ahead of time and discuss their job as observers, showing them how to put checks onto the form each time a group member exhibits the identified skill. Since they will have seen you performing this role many times, they'll catch on quickly.

Remember also to show them how to give feedback by *describing* what they have seen, not evaluating it. Even though students also will have seen you do this repeatedly, some students tend to make judgments unless they're reminded not to.

Student Learning From Observer Role

Students learn a lot by being observers, including just how difficult it is to capture everything that happens. If they receive complaints ("But I contributed my ideas more than *once*!" or "You didn't notice when I complimented Joey!"), student observers are helped to understand that *you* can't notice everything they do in *their* groups.

Also, if students are having a problem working in groups, being an observer gives them an opportunity to see the behavior they need to acquire—especially if you ask them to observe particularly effective groups.

A special lesson for students who tend to dominate groups can occur when they take the role of observer: they have a chance to see groups functioning perfectly well without their contributions. (One such student commented,"I wanted to show them how to solve the problem, but I made myself keep quiet, and they actually figured it out!")

Other Benefits—and One Caveat

Using student observers can also solve the problem of what to do with a student whose partner is absent for a paired activity.

And students think it's fun!

But remember: since the observer doesn't participate in the activity, she or he has to "catch up" on the material being discussed. Sometimes this can be done simply by allowing five minutes at the end of the lesson for each group to bring the observer up to speed. Sometimes—if you have just one student observer—you can do the catching up later, while another activity is going on.

Rewarding and Reinforcing Social Skill Achievement

In Chapter 5 we encouraged you to reward students' success in learning social skills just as you reward their academic success, and we noted that putting a star on a group's paper after you had observed them for a few minutes was one quick way to reinforce their efforts. (You may prefer drawing a happy face or writing "Super!" or doing something else.)

To emphasize the importance of social skills, you can set goals for success just as you do with an academic task: "If everyone in your group makes at least one encouraging statement and contributes at least one idea to the discussion while I am observing, you each earn a sticker."

But we think you'll find that simply noticing students' use of social skills becomes a sufficient reward in most cases.

- "Winnie, I saw you encouraging Sally to explain her ideas and helping her clarify her thoughts. She seemed pleased to be included in the discussion."
  "Liz, I heard you paraphrasing Michael's contribution to be sure you understood. That really helped John understand, too."
  "While I watched your group, you seemed to be working very well together:

each of you complimented the others, and you all listened without interrupting."

The reason you don't have to give lots of stickers and stars and grades for students' use of social skills is that students quickly find that they like using those skills—once they get over the initial embarrassment or awkwardness. They like complimenting others—and being complimented. They learn to like listening, especially since they know they'll be listened to. They enjoy saying encouraging words and having group mates encourage them. Eventually they even like giving up put-downs and knowing that their group will be a safe, friendly place where they don't have to fear being insulted or made to feel inadequate. And those who are old enough to engage in Higher-Order Thinking Skills find them challenging and satisfying.

> Some people are funny and some are serious. I learned that people are different and I can work with all of them.
>
> — Student

Our Best Advice

We have described several ways you can help students become conscious and effective users of social skills. We're sure you'll think of others. What we can't emphasize enough is the need for you to emphasize the importance of these skills to your students.

Persevere. Don't be discouraged if your students are self-conscious and sound "phony" at first. They will until they get used to using these new skills. But their efforts—and yours—will be worth it.

Solving Problems

"What kinds of difficulties am I likely to have with cooperative learning groups? Are there problems I can avoid?"

T here are three potential sources of problems for teachers using cooperative learning groups: students, other adults (teachers, administrators, parents), and their own eagerness to get going.

We think you can avoid many problems with advance planning, but other problems may well be unavoidable. This chapter describes problems that may come from each of the three sources and gives our best advice for preventing those problems if possible, or handling them successfully if they arise.

Problems With Students

"What do I do with a student who refuses to participate in cooperative group activities?"

Preventive Tactics

1. You can help avoid having reluctant students by emphasizing to your class that groups aren't permanent and that everyone will have a chance to work with everyone else.

2. It's also important to let youngsters know that they are expected to get along in their groups, and that nonfunctional groups will stay together until they *can* function well. (This counteracts students' expectations that if they don't like their present group members, all they have to do is refuse to get along and you'll put them into a different group.)

Possible Solutions

1. Sometimes it helps to coach a reluctant (or recalcitrant) student ahead of time on just what will be expected in the group. Be sure to sound positive and encouraging—as if you are sure he or she will participate, even if you're not.

2. Use an observation sheet with individual names on it and give immediate positive reinforcement for any close approximation of the social skill you have asked for: stop the group and show the check(s) you have made. Often these children are desperate for recognition and will respond eagerly when they see the checks they can earn.

3. Treat this as a problem belonging to the group, and enlist everyone's help in solving it. Sit with the group and ask other group members what they can do to encourage the reluctant student. Ask the student what would help him or her participate.

4. If nothing works, offer the student the option of doing the entire assignment individually. It's amazing how well this strategy works to get most

reluctant students back into their group, since they are quick to see that two heads are better than one.

"What do I do about a student nobody wants in a group because of his or her behavior problems?"

Preventive Tactics

1. If you have access to a social worker, guidance counselor, or school psychologist, enlist that professional's help in designing a behavior modification strategy to enable this student to function reasonably well within a group.

2. If you don't have any support people available, have a conference with the student and either coach him or her on one skill you think will help or give a pep talk about how much fun he or she will have working with classmates. In either case we encourage you to be direct. Start your conversation with an acknowledgment of the problem: "Gordon, I know you haven't been as successful as you'd like to be working in your group..." or "Cynthia, I know you haven't yet enjoyed working in a group...." Then move on to either identifying the skill you think will enable the student to be more successful or describing the reasons you think she or he will come to enjoy group work.

Possible Solutions

1. Offer support to the group by giving an extra reward (bonus points, sticker, and so on) for working with the student. You don't have to do this secretly, although you may choose to. In many cases it's a good idea to be up front about the difficulty with the student and the group. You can say something like "Martin and Cathy, you know that Susie is learning how to wait her turn and work with others, and sometimes this is difficult for her. I think that you two can help her, but I know this will take extra effort on your part. So I will give you each an extra sticker for being patient with Susie and helping her work with you."

- Sometimes teachers respond to this suggestion with horror. "But that would be embarrassing for Susie!" Our experience suggests that, on the contrary, Susie is likely to be relieved to learn that her partners will be rewarded for working with her, because she knows she tends to blow up, and that other students don't want her in their groups for that reason. Remember, if a student is disliked because of his or her behavior problems, those problems—and that dislike—are not a secret!

2. Intervene and be as directive with a misbehaving student as you would

"Perhaps the most important psychological outcome of cooperative learning methods is their [positive] effect on students' self-esteem,"

Robert E. Slavin. *Cooperative Learning: Theory, Research, and Practice.* Englewood Cliffs, N.J.: Prentice Hall, 1990. Page 43.

normally be. Remind him or her of your expectations. (You'll find that you'll need to intervene in various groups from time to time to help with social and academic problems. Don't worry about knowing when you're needed—it will be obvious that the students have hit a roadblock.)

3. If necessary, remove the student from the group for that lesson, stating that she or he will have another chance the next time the group gets together. Reward the other students for their efforts.

"How do I handle absentees?"

Preventive Tactics

1. If a student is chronically absent, offer his or her group members a reward if they can get the student to come in and complete the assignment. Often if a classmate calls and says, "We need you. Can't you come to school tomorrow?" a student will make an effort to come.

Possible Solutions

1. If one member of a pair is absent, make the remaining student an observer. Or, put him or her with another absentee's partner if the activity is not a long-term assignment.

2. If two members of a trio are present, reapportion the assignment fairly.

3. If the assignment is a long-term project, and the group needs the work of the missing member, have the group call the student at home and ask about the work. (You call, too, to find out when the student is coming in.)

Always have students bring group members up to speed when they return from an absence. If there's homework to be done, you can even tell group members that they are responsible for calling their absent partners and giving them the assignment.

"I'd like to use group grades to promote interdependence, but I'm sure my students—and their parents—will object. What should I do?"

Preventive Tactics

1. As we said in Chapter 4, group grades work best for activities in which students see clearly that it is impossible for you to determine just what each person contributed to the final product. If you decide that it is appropriate to give a group grade for a project, explain carefully to your students just why they will all be earning the same grade and what the criteria are for the grade that will be earned.

2. When giving a group grade, provide opportunities for students to demonstrate their own learning through individual tests or essays.

Possible Solutions

1. Avoid group grades and use other strategies to promote positive interdependence until your students are comfortable working in cooperative groups and feel sure that each group member will pull his or her own weight.

One strategy that helps students become interested in the quality of their partners' work is to give bonus points to all group members if each person in the group completes his or her part of the project and achieves the minimum criterion you have established for success.

"What should I do if my high-achieving students don't want to work in groups because they think their grades will suffer?"

Preventive Tactics

1. Before putting your students into cooperative learning groups, take time to describe the importance of learning to work together. Share with them the 1982 research finding of the Center for Public Resources[1] : ninety percent of people fired from their jobs are fired for poor attitudes and poor interpersonal skills. Assure them that they will learn social skills in their cooperative groups that will help them be successful in whatever work they choose to do as adults.

2. Explain that they will learn more than they expect because teaching others helps them understand their own knowledge better.

3. Reassure them that their grades won't suffer—provided they help their group mates learn the material.

4. Make it worth their while: give bonus points if everyone in their group reaches a certain criterion. Since high-achieving students are grade-conscious, they love being able to get a grade higher than 100.

Possible Solutions

The solutions for dealing with resistant high-achieving students are the same as the preventive tactics: provide plenty of information about why cooperative groups are important for *all* students—including them—and use bonus points to make sure their grades don't suffer.

- One caution: sometimes high-achieving students simply do their own work and ignore their group members. If this happens, their grades *will* suffer because their group members are unlikely to be as successful as you expect. That's OK. Remind the high-achieving students that an important part of group work is being sure their partners understand the material, too. And

"There is no evidence of high-achieving students being 'pulled down' by participating in heterogeneous cooperative groups and considerable evidence that high achievers are 'pushed up,' "

David W. Johnson and Roger T. Johnson. "The High Achieving Student in Heterogeneous Cooperative Learning Groups." (Research report.) University of Minnesota, 1985. Page 2.

1. "Basic Skills in the U.S. Workforce." Center for Public Resources, 1982. Reference: "Social Skills for Successful Group Work." David W. Johnson and Roger T. Johnson. *Educational Leadership* December 1898/January 1990: p.32.

don't back down and reward their individual performance until they are working hard to help their group members.

Problems With Other Adults

"What shall I do if parents complain about my using cooperative learning?"

"Although it may be possible to create tasks on which perform- ance is greater for competitive efforts, the general results of research indicated that cooperation promoted higher achievement on all types of tasks,"

David W. Johnson and Roger T. Johnson. *Coop- eration and Competition: Theory and Research.* Edina, Minn.: Interac- tion Book Com- pany, 1989. Page 172.

Preventive tactics

1. When you first introduce cooperative learning in your classroom, send a letter home, hold an open house, or use a PTA meeting to tell parents just what cooperative learning is and why you think it's so important for their children.

You can anticipate that some parents will be afraid that cooperative learning will make their children unable to compete in the real world. It's important to explain that most jobs in highly competitive firms require people to cooperate with others almost all of the time: the organization tries to out- perform its competitors, but individuals within the organization are expected to work together. Reassure them that you are teaching their children social skills that are essential for success in the real world.

You can also anticipate that some parents of gifted children will think that cooperative groups will hold their children back. Be sure to tell parents that gifted youngsters benefit from cooperative groups, too. Because gifted students often find themselves teaching other students material that comes quickly to them, they learn that material more deeply and understand it better than they would if they were just studying alone for a test. (The "oral rehearsal" of cooperative learning helps them just as much as it does their less gifted classmates.)

Also explain that some gifted children have difficulty making friends, and that cooperative learning not only helps them to develop social skills but also puts them in a setting where they can be appreciated for their abilities, rather then scorned for being a "brain."

Possible Solutions

1. The solution for dealing with complaints from parents is really the same as our suggestion for preventing those complaints: provide information.

If parents ask to have their child removed from a group that the child doesn't like, explain why it is important for students to acquire social skills and why you are insisting that all children stay in a group until they succeed at working together. To help stiffen your resolve, here is a comment from a second grader (whose mother asked to have her removed from a group and be put with her

60

two best friends and whose teacher declined) after a few months of cooperative learning:

- "If you think you don't like someone in your class and you get to work with them, you get to know them better and you learn to like them."

And from an eighth grader:

- "I don't always get along with all the members of my group, but we put our differences aside and get our work done. I like my group a lot, and I'm very comfortable with the people in it."

If parents of a "loner" insist that their child be permitted to work alone, you can assure them that you provide many opportunities for students to work independently and that their child is very successful at that kind of work. But stick to your guns about the importance of helping their child learn to interact with others successfully, too.

> ## "I've been experimenting with cooperative learning, and I'm excited about the results. But I can't seem to get my principal and the other teachers in my building interested."

Preventive Tactics

1. When you first start to use cooperative groups, talk about your efforts with people whose support you would like to have: your principal, of course, and some of your colleagues—perhaps those who are friends or who are on your grade level or whose rooms are nearby. Describe what you're doing and tell them why. Offer to share this book with them.

2. Invite your colleagues to observe a cooperative learning lesson, making them official observers with a sheet for collecting data about student performance. Debrief with them afterward, both to learn what they observed and to explain anything that puzzled them.

Possible Solutions

If your colleagues and principal have declined your invitation to visit and have remained indifferent, you may need to try some roundabout routes.

1. Invite visitors to your building to see cooperative learning—you will arouse others' curiosity.

2. Try to get just one person to partner with you as a "consultant." Ask for

his or her advice, keep inviting him or her to come in and observe, say that you really need his or her help.

3. Put this book and articles about cooperative learning in the teachers' lounge. Talk with others about your successes and your excitement.

4. If your school provides substitutes while you visit other programs, ask to go observe cooperative learning in another school district—preferably one like your own. If your principal realizes that the "competition" is using cooperative learning, she or he may become interested—and you'll also have an opportunity to get ideas from watching someone else use cooperative learning.

5. Join the International Association for the Study of Cooperation in Education.[2] You'll learn about conferences and workshops you can attend—and that you can invite your colleagues to attend with you—and you'll receive a journal devoted to cooperative learning, which you can share with others.

6. Don't give up! So many teachers are using cooperative learning now that your principal and your colleagues are bound to hear about the power of this strategy soon and come to you to learn more about it.

Problems With Yourself

"I'm impatient. I can see the value of cooperative learning, and I want to use it for all my subjects. But I don't have time to plan all the lessons I'd like to teach."

Preventive tactics

There may be no way to prevent feeling impatient. Whenever we decide to learn something new, our desire to be successful quickly is apt to overcome our ability to be patient with ourselves and to allow the natural learning process to take place.

Remember that, as with any new strategy you try, you'll get worse before you get better. Celebrate your victories as they occur. Take the long view.

Possible Solutions

1. Give yourself time. It usually takes a teacher two years to become really adept at using cooperative learning.

2. Set realistic goals for yourself, such as using cooperative learning for just one subject for at least a month or two, until you and your students feel really comfortable with the strategy. Try out different kinds of assignments in that subject. Experiment with ways to build in positive interdependence and

2. Write to IASCE, P.O. Box 1582, Santa Cruz, CA 95061-1582

individual accountability. See what social skills your students need most.

3. Keep plugging. Every good cooperative learning teacher was once a beginner.

"I know it's important for students to evaluate their behavior in their groups, but I have trouble finding the time."

Preventive Tactics

Again, we're not sure there's any way to prevent the feeling of not having enough time. But we have some suggestions for fitting student self-evaluation into each lesson.

Possible Solutions

1. Make the evaluation of group interaction part of the academic task. Add a question to the end of a worksheet or assignment asking students to describe their specific successes as a group and to identify what skill they would like to work on next time. Or ask them to rate themselves as group members and to specify why they gave themselves that rating.

2. At the end of the lesson, ask each student to give a specific example of a successful demonstration of the social skill(s) being practiced that day.

3. Remember the quick check: thumbs up, thumbs down, thumbs sideways. You can vary your questions. (For example, "How well did you work today?" or "How successful were you at encouraging?" or "How would an observer rate you on sticking to the task?")

4. Use a timer. Set it for five or ten minutes before the end of class so that you will be sure to have time for discussing student interactions.

Our Best Advice

At the risk of repeating ourselves, we encourage you to take your time. Enjoy your successes, forgive yourself when things don't go as well as you'd like, and remember: every problem is an opportunity for you—and your students—to learn about cooperation.

In fact, often when things aren't going well in a group (a student doesn't bring his or her work, two students won't take turns, a youngster monopolizes the conversation, no one listens to anyone else), you can turn the problem back to the group: "Your group has a problem. What can you do about it?" Help them generate alternative solutions. You'll be teaching them essential problem-solving skills that will help them to be productive and happy adults.

63

8

Some Recipes

"I'm not very creative. Can't you give me some tried-and-true plans for using cooperative learning?"

Several people have developed structures (or patterns or recipes) for cooperative learning that can be used for a variety of subjects.[1] Once you've learned one of these structures, you can apply it to material that is appropriate to your students. In this chapter we'll describe four structures to give you an idea of the range of activities that can be done cooperatively.

Turn to Your Partner

The simplest structure for cooperative learning is a good way to enliven a whole-class lesson and keep students focused. To prepare students for Turn to Your Partner, tell them that sometimes you will ask them to do some quick work with another student right where they're sitting. Identify how they will know which person is their partner for this quick work.

Whenever you plan to use Turn to Your Partner, tell your students at the start of the lesson to be ready to work with their partner, so they'll be prepared.

At an appropriate point in your lesson, say to your students, "Turn to your partner and... (try to solve this equation; predict whether the cup will sink or float; decide which door Griselda should open)." Give students a minute or two for discussion or problem-solving and then bring their attention back to you. You don't have to ask them to report out to the whole class. Just say something like "Let's see what happens" and go on with your lesson. We predict that you will have them following you eagerly to see if they were right.

You can use Turn to Your Partner throughout a teacher-directed lesson. We think you'll like this structure, because it's an easy way to get students actively engaged with the content you're tying to teach.

To reinforce the use of social skills, you can ask students to shake hands with their partner at the end of the lesson and thank him or her for one specific thing that was helpful.

Think, Pair, Share

Think, Pair, Share is a variation of Turn to Your Partner. Use this structure when you want some or all students to share their ideas with the class.

To introduce students to Think, Pair, Share, you may decide to create a poster to hang in the front of the room:

1. Spencer Kagan, Director of Resources for Teachers, 27134 Paseo Espada, #202, San Juan Capistrano, CA 92675, is a particularly good source for cooperative learning structures.

THINK
PAIR
SHARE

Explain to them that Think, Pair, Share has the following steps:

1. **Think** about the question posed by the teacher. (You may ask older

students to write what they think as the second part of step 1. Or you can teach your students two structures: Think, Pair, Share, and Think, Write, Pair, Share.)

THINK
WRITE
PAIR
SHARE

2. **Pair** with your partner and take turns saying what you think (or reading what you wrote). Discuss your ideas. See if you can come to agreement.
3. **Share** your pair's ideas with the whole class.

For step 3 you can either call on a few of the pairs to get an idea of whether everyone is on the right track or go around the class and have each pair report. If every pair is reporting, it may be appropriate for you (or a student) to keep a tally of the pairs' responses either on a chart or on the blackboard.

Think, Pair, Share takes longer than Turn to Your Partner and is useful for promoting critical thinking about an idea or problem (especially application, analysis, or synthesis).

KWL Columns

KWL Columns is a kind of "bookend" structure: it helps you both to initiate a topic and to bring closure to your students' work on that topic (*see Chart P*).

K W L Chart

K = "What I **Know** About _____."
W = "**What** I Would Like to Learn About _____."
L = "What I Have **Learned** About _____."

K	W	L

Chart P

For a short topic, or for younger children, the KWL columns can all be on the same page.

Older children may have several pages of **L** columns, particularly for a complex topic. For them you may make one page with just **K** and **W** columns and then provide them with as many **L** pages as they need.

First ask students to get into their groups (pairs or trios will work) and talk about what they already know about the topic. As they agree on items, they each write those items in the **K** column on their individual sheets. If one member of the group disagrees about some fact, the person who believes it is true can still write the fact in his or her K column but should add a question mark to indicate that the group doesn't have consensus on the accuracy of this item.

67

For the **W** column you can either have children discuss with their group what they would like to learn and then write their individual lists or have them write their lists alone. The benefit of group discussion is that one child's curiosity about a topic can spark another's interest.

The students' creation of the K and W columns accomplishes three important goals:

> **For very young children who cannot write, KWL can't be done as a cooperative learning activity, but you *can* do it with the whole class. Create KWL columns on a large sheet of news-print or an easel pad, and have the students tell you what to write in the K and then the W columns.**

1. stimulates their interest in the topic
2. provides you with a good diagnostic evaluation of what students know and don't know—or think they know but misunderstand—about the topic
3. gives you clues about how to make the topic interesting to them

Often you'll find yourself adjusting your teaching based on what you read in students' K and W columns.

During or after the lesson(s) on the topic, students can fill in the L column in their groups or alone. If you have them do this work alone, give them time to get back into their groups and compare their learnings.

Be sure to have your students compare their L and K columns: often they discover that what they thought they knew turned out to be inaccurate or incomplete.

With KWL Columns you can use any of the strategies for promoting the social skill development that we discussed in Chapter 6.

Pick Your Spot

Pick Your Spot is a good structure for getting students to identify and declare their beliefs or opinions and then explore them with like-minded classmates. Spencer Kagan calls this structure Corners.[2] We call it Pick Your Spot, because we like to provide more than four choices for students.

The structure has the following steps:

- 1. You ask a question that calls for students to select from a number of options. For example, "If you could do one of these activities for an hour, which would you pick: reading a book you like, playing Nintendo, watching TV, playing a game outside with your friends, going for a walk alone, or doing something with your mother or father or other adult?"

(Choices given can also be related to a curriculum topic or a problem the class is trying to solve. "Which of the following is the most important article the Pilgrims brought with them?" "Which of the following is the best

2. See Kagan's "The Structural Approach to Cooperative Learning." *Educational Leadership.* December 1989/January 1990: p. 14.

solution to our problem with people not returning materials they have borrowed?")

- 2. Identify the "spots" in the room for people holding each of the alternatives you have identified. (You can identify any number of alternatives. Some questions will legitimately have six to eight; some may have just three or four.) Ask students to quickly and quietly Pick Your Spot.

- 3. Tell students to discuss their choice with the people in their spot, and see how many good reasons they can generate for their position. Tell them each group member should be prepared to share their reasoning with the rest of the class and see if their group can gain any converts.

- 4. After allowing time for discussion (and monitoring the groups while they talk about their reasons for their position), call on one student from each group to describe that group's position. After all groups have reported out, ask if any students would now like to change their position and pick a new spot. If any do, ask them to say which argument persuaded them.

Variations on Pick Your Spot

You can experiment with different instructions for Pick Your Spot. For example, in step 3 you can appoint recorders for each group to take notes and report the group's reasons for choosing that option. Step 4 can be expanded to include questions and/or challenges from members in other groups. (Questions should be for information and clarification. Challenges should be questions about the group's logic or the information it used to make its decision.)

You can also go through two rounds of Pick Your Spot. After step 4, change your question slightly or give the students some additional information and ask them to rethink their position. Then tell them to pick their spot again—either by staying in place or moving to another spot.

Our Best Advice

As you explore cooperative learning, you'll discover many structures and approaches to follow. We encourage you to concentrate on a few that work well for you, but we also encourage you to keep looking for alternatives. Sometimes the class you have one year responds well to one approach, while next year's class needs something different.

Get ideas from your colleagues. See if you can form a support group of teachers using cooperative learning, and meet over lunch, or before school, or even (occasionally) during the evening. (Some teachers create a "cooperative feast" for their support group meetings.) Exchange lesson plans, help each other with problems as they arise, and—above all—give each other lots of encouragement.

As we have said repeatedly, take your time, but keep adding to your repertoire of cooperative learning strategies. The more you know about this approach to teaching and learning, the more we think you will want to know.

> **When you grow up and you're in a big corporation and someone has a stupid idea, instead of saying, "I hate the idea," you'll say, "That's a good idea, but here's another," or, "Let's look at our options," or "Are there other possibilities?"**
>
> — Student

Recommended Materials

Books

Davidson, N. (Ed.). *Cooperative Learning in Mathematics.* N.Y.: Addison-Wesley, 1990.

Gaylord-Ross, R. (Ed.) *Interaction Strategies for Students With Handicaps.* Baltimore: Paul H. Brookes Publishers, 1989.

Johnson, D.W. *Cooperation and Competition: Theory and Research.* Edina, Minn.: Interaction Book Company, 1989.

Johnson, D.W. *Leading the Cooperative School.* Edina, Minn.: Interaction Book Company, 1988.

Johnson, D.W., R.T. Johnson, and E.J. Holubec. *Circles of Learning: Cooperation in the Classroom* (revised). Edina, Minn.: Interaction Book Company, 1986.

Periodicals

Cooperative Learning. Vol .10, No. 3. March 1990.

Educational Leadership. Vol. 47, No. 4. December 1989/January 1990: pp. 4-67. (Cooperative Learning Issue.)

Teaching Materials

Dishon, D., and P.W. O'Leary. *A Guidebook for Cooperative Learning: A Technique for Creating More Effective Schools.* Holmes Beach, Fla.: Learning Publications, Inc., 1984.

Johnson, D.W., and R.T. Johnson. *Structuring Cooperative Learning: Lesson Plans for Teachers.* Edina, Minn.: Interaction Book Company, 1985.

Schniedewind, N., and E. Davidson. *Cooperative Learning, Cooperative Lives.* Dubuque, Iowa: Wm. C. Brown Company Publishers, 1987.

Movies

Johnson, D.W., and R.T. Johnson (Producers). *Circles of Learning.* Edina, Minn.: Interaction Book Company, 1983.

Videotapes

Cooperative Learning. Alexandria, VA: Association for Supervision and Curriculum Development, 1990.

Susan S. Ellis started investigating cooperative learning teaching strategies in 1983. As coordinator of staff development for the Greenwich, Connecticut Public Schools, she gives training programs and workshops on cooperative learning and other teaching strategies. She is also a member of the board of overseers of the Regional Laboratory for Educational Improvement of the Northeast and the Islands.

Susan writes a column on the role of the principal in professional development for *The Journal of Staff Development;* she also writes regularly for various other professional publications.

In December 1990, she received the Distinguished Service Award from the National Staff Development Council.

Susan F. Whalen teaches elementary school students in Connecticut. Her fifth-grade class was the subject of a cooperative learning videotape published by the Association for Supervision and Curriculum Development. Susan has trained extensively with Roger, David, and Edythe Johnson. She conducts workshops on cooperative learning teaching strategies. Susan says, "The workshops give me fresh ideas and send me back to my classroom with renewed energy."